W9-BSV-006

I Love to Draw Horses!

Jennifer Lipsey

LARK BOOKS
A Division of Sterling Publishing Co,. Inc.
New York / London

My Very Favorite Art Book

This book is dedicated to kids who love art and horses.

Editor
VERONIKA ALICE GUNTER

Creative Director
CELIA NARANJO

Production Assistant
BRADLEY NORRIS

Library of Congress Cataloging-in-Publication Data

Lipsey, Jennifer.
  I love to draw horses! / by Jennifer Lipsey. -- 1st ed.
      p. cm. -- (My very favorite art book)
  Includes index.
  ISBN-13: 978-1-60059-152-5 (hc-plc with jacket : alk. paper)
  ISBN-10: 1-60059-152-3 (hc-plc with jacket : alk. paper)
  1. Horses in art--Juvenile literature. 2. Drawing--Technique--Juvenile literature. I. Title.
  NC783.8.H65L57 2008
  743.6'96655--dc22

                                    2007049048
10 9 8 7 6 5 4 3 2 1

First Edition

Published by Lark Books, A Division of
Sterling Publishing Co., Inc.
387 Park Avenue South, New York, NY 10016

© 2008, Jennifer Lipsey

Distributed in Canada by Sterling Publishing,
c/o Canadian Manda Group, 165 Dufferin Street
Toronto, Ontario, Canada M6K 3H6

Distributed in the United Kingdom by GMC Distribution Services,
Castle Place, 166 High Street, Lewes, East Sussex, England BN7 1XU

Distributed in Australia by Capricorn Link (Australia) Pty Ltd.,
P.O. Box 704, Windsor, NSW 2756 Australia

If you have questions or comments about this book, please contact:

Lark Books
67 Broadway
Asheville, NC 28801
828-253-0467

Manufactured in China

ISBN 13: 978-1-60059-152-5
ISBN 10: 1-60059-152-3

For information about custom editions, special sales, premium and corporate purchases, please contact Sterling Special Sales Department at 800-805-5489 or specialsales@sterlingpub.com.

Contents

The Horse is a very special animal!

No other animal in history has inspired more artwork!

People have been drawing, painting, and carving pictures of horses for thousands of years.

This book will help you become the horse artist you have always wanted to be!

This book will help you draw different horses.

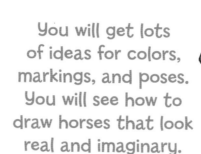

You will get lots of ideas for colors, markings, and poses. You will see how to draw horses that look real and imaginary.

You will learn to draw different riders.

You will see what it looks like to put your horse in a scene.

Drawing Horses is fun!

1. 2. 3.

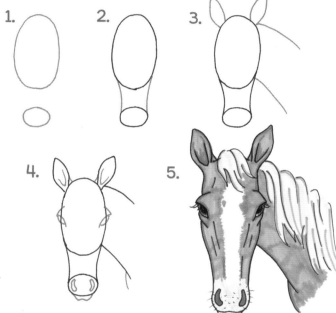

4. 5.

This book will help you draw beautiful horses. It is also very good to practice drawing from real horses when you can.

You just need paper and pencil to get started.

It will be helpful to have an eraser, black felt-tip pen, and something to color with, such as markers, crayons, or colored pencils.

It's not hard, but it does take PRACTICE! Don't worry if your drawings don't look like the ones in this book. Just have fun!

Here are what the steps look like in this book. The PINK lines show each step.

How about a Blue Ribbon for your winning horse?

Here are the steps to finish your drawings:

1. Use a pencil to follow the steps for drawing a horse. Draw lightly!

2. Go over the lines you want to keep with a black pen or marker.

3. Erase all the leftover lines.

4. Color your horse!

What a beauty!

Now Let's Draw Horses!

Horse Parts

Knowing the parts of a horse
will make drawing it easier.

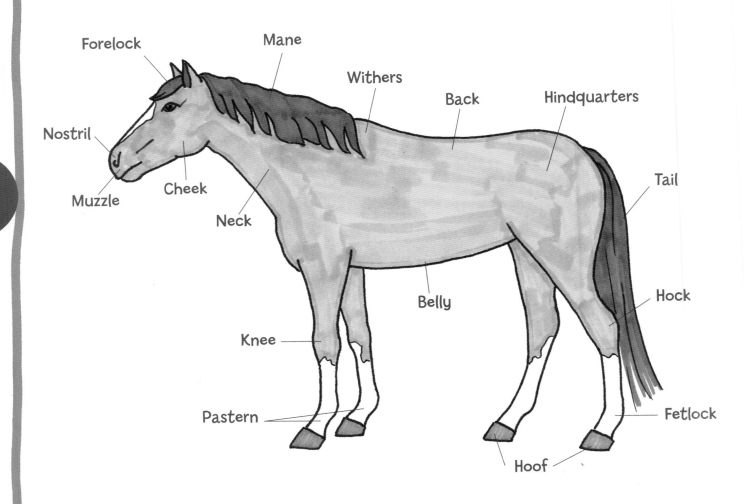

Forelock

Mane

Withers

Back

Hindquarters

Nostril

Tail

Muzzle

Cheek

Neck

Belly

Hock

Knee

Pastern

Fetlock

Hoof

Horse Tack

Tack is the special equipment a horse wears so a rider can control it.

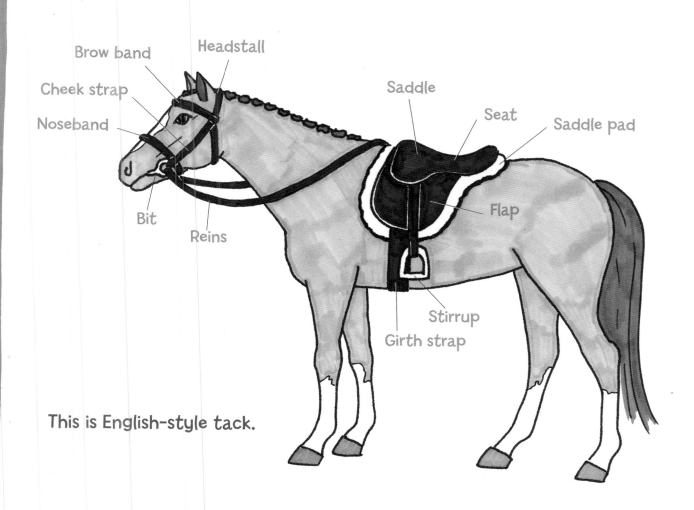

Brow band

Headstall

Cheek strap

Saddle

Seat

Noseband

Saddle pad

Bit

Flap

Reins

Stirrup

Girth strap

This is English-style tack.

Ready to ride?

Basic Horse

1.

Draw circles and ovals for the body and neck.

2.

Add circles for the leg joints and the head.

3.

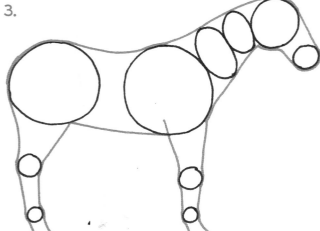

Outline the horse's shape. Draw extra lines on the ends of the legs for pasterns.

4.

Erase the circles and ovals. Draw the tail, hooves, mane, and face.

Try drawing your horse looking the other way.

Draw the kind of mane, tail, and markings you want your horse to have.

Try drawing a horse with four legs showing.

Foals

A foal is a young horse. A female foal is called a filly.
A male foal is called a colt. Foals have long legs, big eyes,
and a short mane and tail.

1.

Draw two circles for the body.
The second circle is a little
bigger than the first.

2.

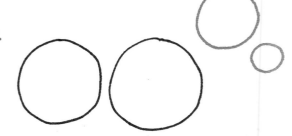

Now draw circles for the
leg joints and the head.

3.

Trace around the
circles to draw
the body and
legs. Add short
lines for the
pasterns.

4.

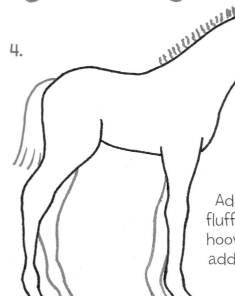

Add a short tail and
fluffy mane. Draw ears,
hooves, and a face. Try
adding two more legs.

Front-Facing Foal

13

Draw your filly or colt with its mother to show how small the foal is.

Horse Colors

Horses come in many colors.
These are just a few.

GRAY
Light gray, with or without spots

CHESTNUT
Deep reddish brown with mane
and tail the same color

DUN
Tan with a black mane and tail

BAY
Red to dark brown with a black mane and tail

PALOMINO
Golden or tan with a pale or white mane and tail

PINTO
Large patches of white and another color. A pinto is also called a paint. Can you see why?

You can make your horse any color you want.

Face Markings

A face marking is a white shape
on a darker-colored horse.

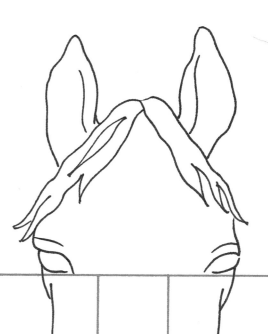

Star

A star is any white marking
between or above the eyes.

Stripe

A stripe is a narrow line
down the middle of
the face. It's also called
a strip or a race.

Snip

A snip is a marking on the
muzzle, between the nostrils.

You can combine stars, stripes, and snips to
make every horse you draw look different.

Make your horse look special by drawing face markings.

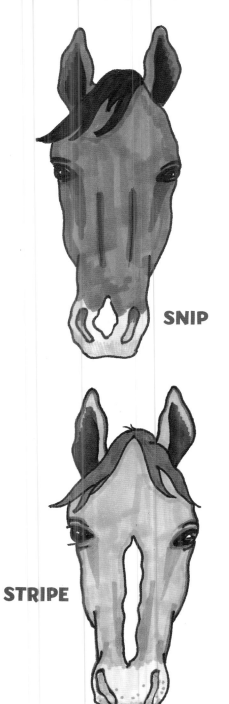

SNIP

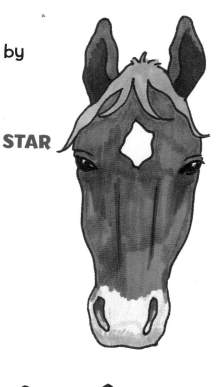

STAR

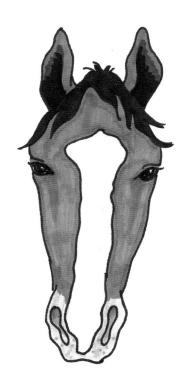

BLAZE

A blaze is a wide white stripe down the middle of the face.
(star + stripe + snip)

STRIPE

BALD

A bald face is a very wide blaze.

Horse Portraits

Front View

1.

2.

3.
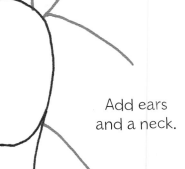

Add ears and a neck.

4.
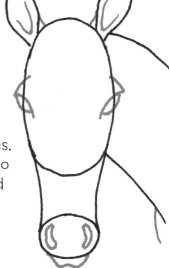

Now draw eyes. Add details to the ears and muzzle.

5.
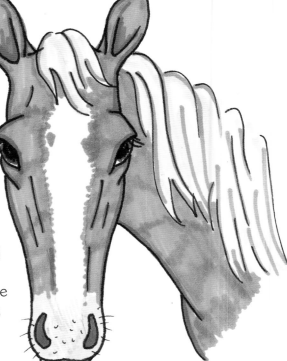

Draw a mane and forelock, eyelashes, and whiskers. Add lines on the face to show bones and muscles.

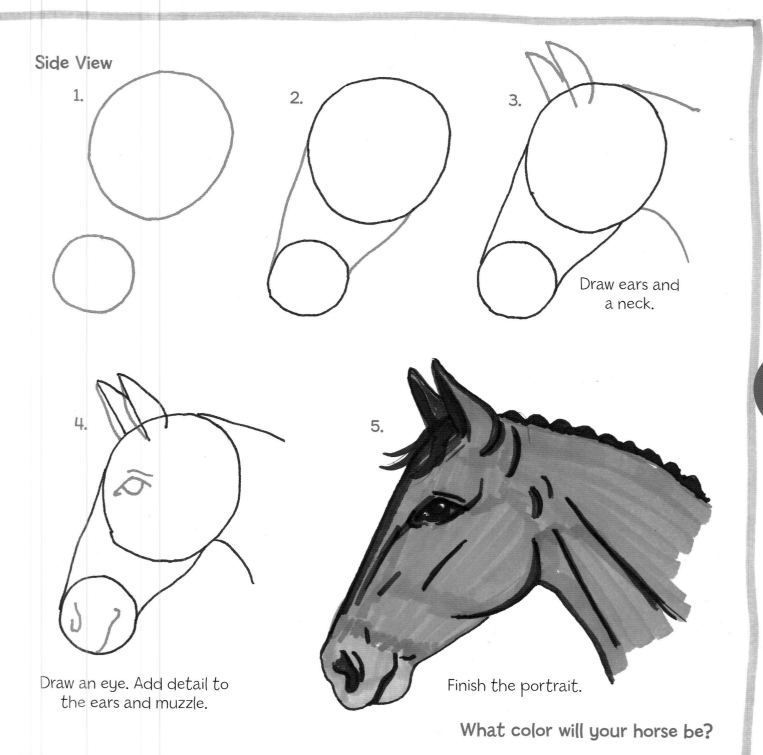

Side View

1.

2.

3. Draw ears and a neck.

4. Draw an eye. Add detail to the ears and muzzle.

5. Finish the portrait.

What color will your horse be?

19

Grazing Horse

1.

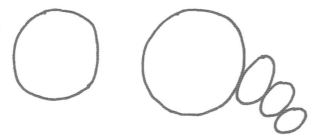

Draw circles for the body.
Draw three ovals for the neck.

2.

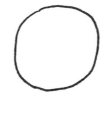

Add circles for
the head and
the joints.

3.

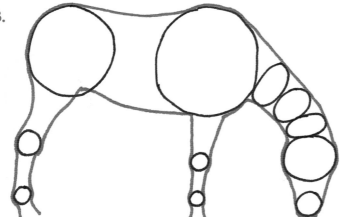

Outline the body. Add
short lines for the pasterns.

4.

Draw the face and ears. Add a mane, tail,
and hooves. Add two more legs if you want.

How about a pretty pink morning sky?

Try drawing your
horse reflected
in water.

Lying Down Horse

Horses lie down when they feel safe and want to rest.

1.

Draw circle and ovals for the body and head.

2.

Trace around the body and head. Draw circles for the leg joints.

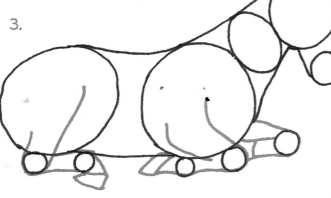

3.

Now draw the legs and hooves.

4.

Add the ears, forelock, mane, face details, and tail.

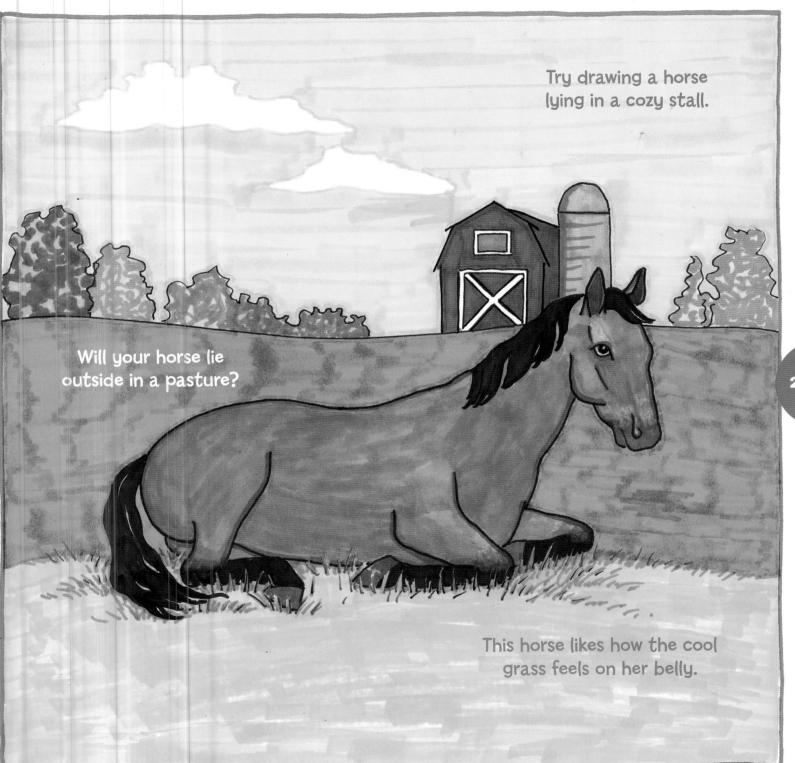

Try drawing a horse lying in a cozy stall.

Will your horse lie outside in a pasture?

This horse likes how the cool grass feels on her belly.

Arabian

The beautiful Arabian is the oldest and purest breed of horses.

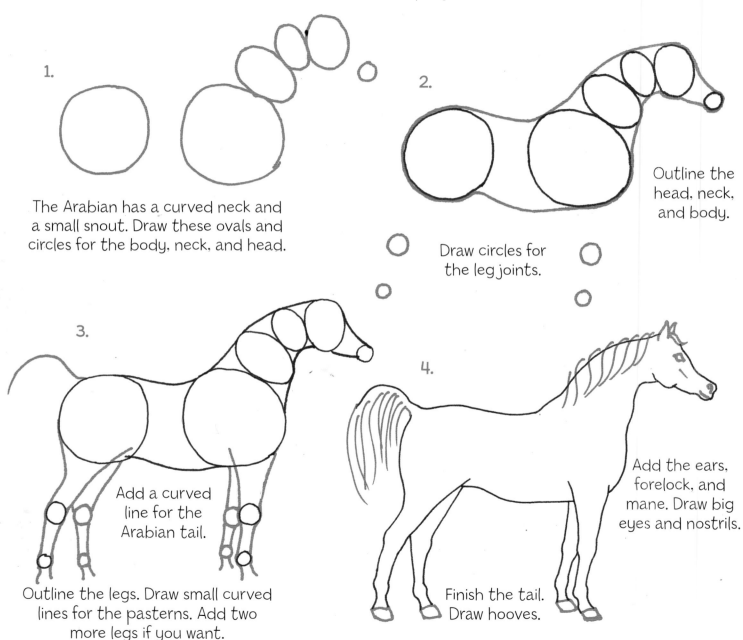

1. The Arabian has a curved neck and a small snout. Draw these ovals and circles for the body, neck, and head.

2. Outline the head, neck, and body. Draw circles for the leg joints.

3. Add a curved line for the Arabian tail. Outline the legs. Draw small curved lines for the pasterns. Add two more legs if you want.

4. Add the ears, forelock, and mane. Draw big eyes and nostrils. Finish the tail. Draw hooves.

Arabian horses are bay, gray, chestnut, brown, and sometimes black.

Try drawing the mane and tail blowing in the wind.

You can draw your horse anywhere you want. Why not at the beach?

Draft Horse

A draft horse is very big, strong, and tall. It's used for heavy work, such as pulling.

1.

Draft horses have thick necks and bodies. Draw these circles and ovals for the body, neck, and head.

2.

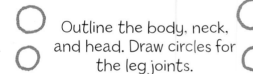

Outline the body, neck, and head. Draw circles for the leg joints.

3.

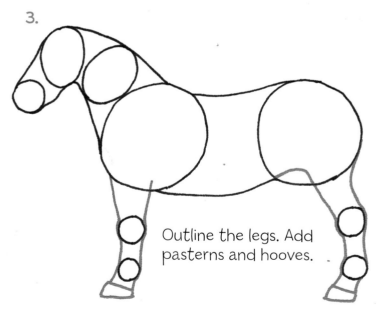

Outline the legs. Add pasterns and hooves.

4.

Draw two more legs if you want.

Finish your horse. Add fringes of hair on the legs.

A draft horse can haul a heavy wagon, pull a plow, or even a sleigh! Jingle bells, jingle bells...

Try drawing lines on the body to show muscles.

Draft horses sometimes have long hair on their legs. This is called feathering.

Draft horses are called coldblooded because their ancestors are from cold climates.

Appaloosa

The Appaloosa is a spotted horse. It's one of the oldest and most popular breeds. Here are some Appaloosa coat patterns:

Frost

White specks all over (Try drawing lots of scribbles.)

Leopard

White body with dark spots

Blanket

White rear with or without spots

Snowflake

White spots over the rear

The Nez Percé tribe bred the Appaloosa horse in the 18th century.

Cave paintings of spotted horses date back 20,000 years.

Appaloosas can have more than one coat pattern at the same time.

Learn to draw a foal on page 12.

Shetland Pony

A pony is a small horse. The Shetland pony has a round body and short legs. Its ancestors come from the Shetland Islands of Scotland.

1.

Draw these circles for the body and a wide oval for the neck.

2.

Add circles for the joints and the head.

3.

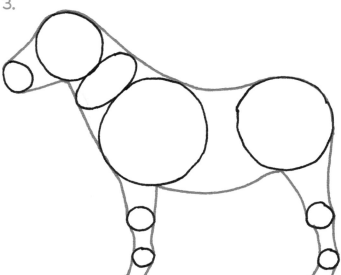

Outline your pony. Add short lines for the pasterns. Draw hooves.

4.

Add a fluffy forelock, mane, and tail.

Draw the face details and ears.

Show two more legs if you want.

Draw a big fence to show
how small your pony is.

What color will your pony be?
What markings will it have?

Rearing Horse

A horse is rearing when it stands up on its hind legs.

1.

Draw circles for the head and body.

2.

Add circles for the leg joints.

3.

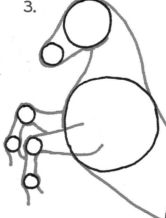

Outline the body.

Draw short lines for the pasterns.

4.

Add face details and ears. Draw the forelock, mane, tail, and hooves.

Try Drawing a Horse Silhouette

1. Draw your horse.
2. Color the sky and sunset.
3. Color everything else solid black.

Walk

A gait is the style and speed that a horse moves. The walk is the slowest gait. The horse's feet hit the ground one at a time.

1.

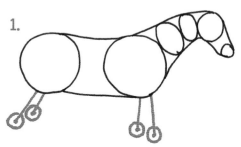

Draw the body. Add stick lines for the upper legs. Add circles for the knee joints.

2.

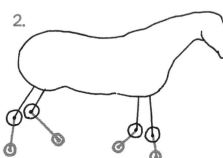

Draw lines and circles for the lower legs and fetlocks.

3.

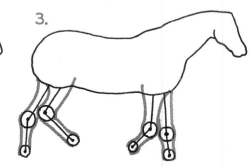

Outline the legs.

4.

Draw pasterns and hooves. Add a mane, tail, forelock, ears, and face.

5.

Where is your horse walking? On a trail? In a pasture? On the beach?

—Walking

Trot

The trot is a faster gait than the walk. The horse's feet hit the ground in pairs. The front foot and opposite back foot move at the same time.

1.
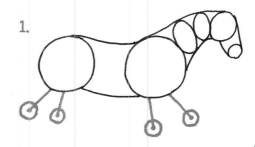
Draw the body. Add stick lines for the upper legs. These lines angle away from each other. Add circles for the knee joints.

2.
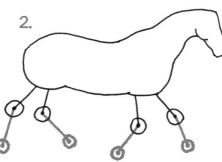
Draw lines and circles for the lower legs and fetlocks.

3.
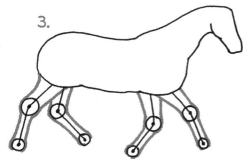
Outline the legs.

4.

Draw pasterns and hooves. Add a mane, tail, ears, and face.

5.

Make this horse a pinto. See page 15.

— Trotting

Canter

The canter gait is faster than a trot but slower than a gallop.

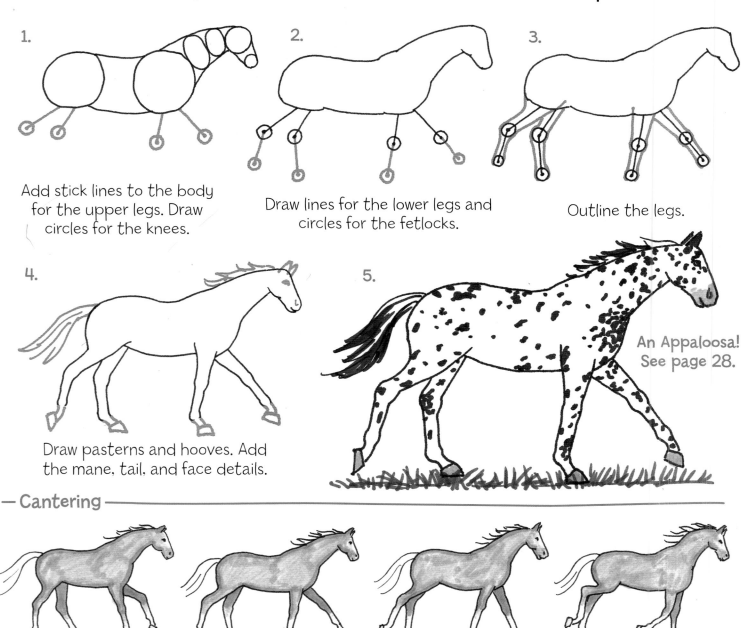

1.
Add stick lines to the body for the upper legs. Draw circles for the knees.

2.
Draw lines for the lower legs and circles for the fetlocks.

3.
Outline the legs.

4.
Draw pasterns and hooves. Add the mane, tail, and face details.

5.
An Appaloosa! See page 28.

— Cantering

Gallop

The gallop is the fastest way a horse moves. All four feet are off the ground at the same time once in each stride.

1.

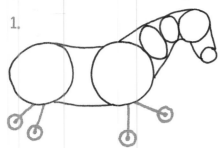

Draw lines and circles for the upper legs and knees.

2.

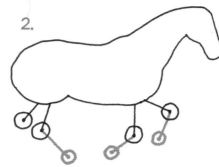

Draw lines for the lower legs and circles for the fetlocks.

3.

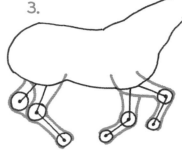

One back leg is behind the other.

Outline the legs.

4.

Add pasterns, hooves, ears, and face details. Draw the mane and tail flying out behind the horse. This horse is moving fast!

Try drawing dirt flying up.

— Galloping —

Horse & Rider

Use this book to draw any horse you want. Then draw this simple rider. The rider could be YOU!

1.

Draw the rider's upper leg.

2.

Add the upper body.

Draw the lower leg.

3.

Draw the neck and head. Add the arm and hand.

4.

Draw a saddle. Add a rein and stirrup.

Finish your rider any way you like.

All of these riders started out as the same basic pony and person.

Elf Maiden

Cowgirl
(Western Style)

Princess

English
Style

American
Indian

Racehorse

A racehorse has a long, lean, muscular body. It stretches out with each stride to cover as much ground as possible. Here is how to draw a jockey on a racehorse:

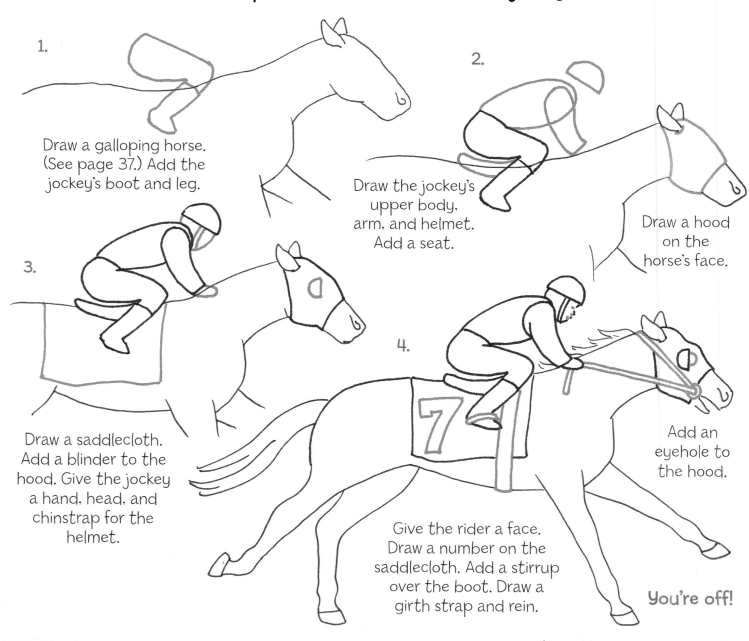

1. Draw a galloping horse. (See page 37.) Add the jockey's boot and leg.

2. Draw the jockey's upper body, arm, and helmet. Add a seat.

Draw a hood on the horse's face.

3. Draw a saddlecloth. Add a blinder to the hood. Give the jockey a hand, head, and chinstrap for the helmet.

Add an eyehole to the hood.

4. Give the rider a face. Draw a number on the saddlecloth. Add a stirrup over the boot. Draw a girth strap and rein.

You're off!

People have been racing horses for thousands of years. Thoroughbreds have been bred and trained to be the world's fastest racehorses.

Try coloring a bright pattern on the jockey's silks (his clothes).

Use matching colors for the horse's hood.

How about drawing a big scene with lots of horses racing?

41

Jumping

Show jumping is the sport of riding horses over obstacles such as fences.

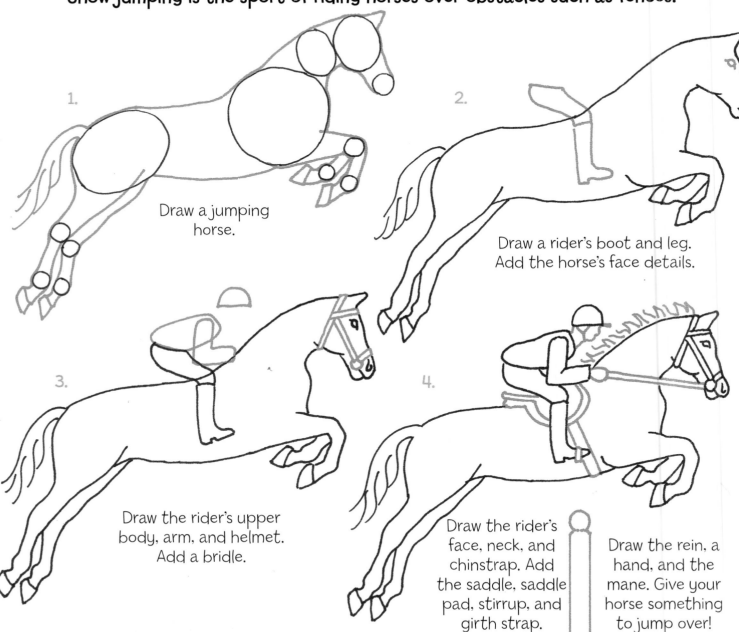

1. Draw a jumping horse.

2. Draw a rider's boot and leg. Add the horse's face details.

3. Draw the rider's upper body, arm, and helmet. Add a bridle.

4. Draw the rider's face, neck, and chinstrap. Add the saddle, saddle pad, stirrup, and girth strap.

Draw the rein, a hand, and the mane. Give your horse something to jump over!

Try drawing the mane flying. This makes it look like the horse is really jumping through the air.

How about drawing some lines on your horse's body to show its muscles?

There are many different types of jumps. Try drawing a fence, a log, or a wall for your horse to jump over.

How high can your horse jump?

Unicorn

There are many ancient legends about the unicorn. It looks
like a horse with a long, twisting horn on its forehead.

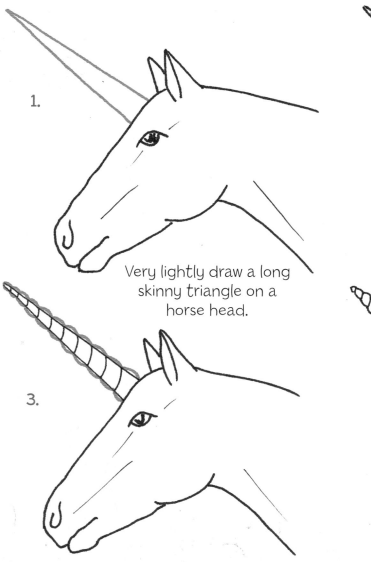

1. Very lightly draw a long
skinny triangle on a
horse head.

3. Connect the curved lines with small
bumps to make a twisting horn.

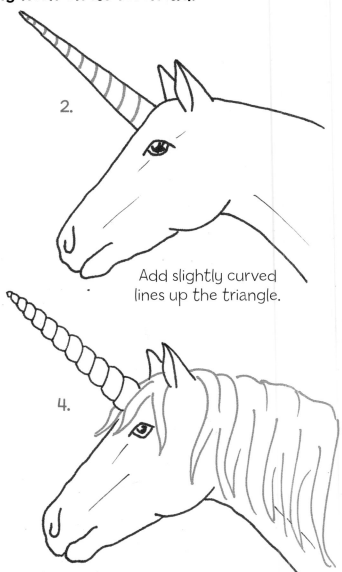

2. Add slightly curved
lines up the triangle.

4. Add a forelock and a mane.
It's a beautiful unicorn!

Where will your unicorn live?

Winged Horse

The winged horse is a creature from mythology. The most famous winged horse is named Pegasus.

1.

Draw a galloping horse. (See page 37.)

2.

Lightly draw a wing shape coming from the horse's withers.

3.

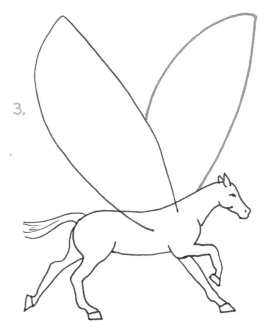

Add a second wing behind the first.

4.

Draw feathers on the wings.

Add a fluffy, flying mane.

Fly high!

Make your
winged horse
any color
you want.

Draw land far below
to show how high your
horse is flying.

Acknowledgments

This is a quote from a beautifully illustrated card I received from a 7-year-old student named Anna:

> Thank you for being my art teacher. Art is my favorite subejet. I rilly like art. I like all the tricks you teach me. They all work.

Although I can't be every kid's personal art teacher, I hope to encourage, inspire, and "teach tricks" to lots of kids through this book and my other books. I feel blessed to play a part in nurturing kids' creativity. And it is fun to imagine kids all over the world proudly declaring "I rilly like art!"

I would like to acknowledge the hard-working folks at Lark Books, especially Veronika and Celia. Special thanks to my Aunt Maureen for sharing her knowledge and love of horses. I would also like to thank Victoria, one of my Summer Art Camp students, for her valuable critique of one of the first spreads I did for this book.

My friends and family have been so supportive and encouraging and I am grateful.

I am inspired by my baby Oliver to create quality work so that he too might enjoy it and be proud of his Mama when he is older. As always, I thank Martin for his love and the expertly brewed hot tea, stories, and diaper changes for Oliver while I worked.

Lastly, I give thanks to the Great Creator who always provides ideas and solutions just when I think there aren't any more to be had.

Index